The publication is generously sponsored

by Iris & Junming Le Foundation

OARS OVER WHITECAPS

Selected Works of American Chinese Poets

Translated by Denis Mair

Edited by Yan Li & Paul Qiu

I Wing Press • New York

OARS OVER WHITECAPS

Selected Works of American Chinese Poets

Translator: Denis Mair

Editor: Yan Li & Paul Qiu

Published by I Wing Press, New York

Book Designer: Alex Wang

2025.4, First Edition, First Printing

ISBN: 978-1-961768-15-4

Price: $19.95

Brief Biography of the Translator

Denis Mair (梅丹理) holds an M.A. in Chinese from Ohio State University and has taught as lecturer at Whitman College and University of Pennsylvania. He was a research fellow for many years at Hanching Academy (Sun Moon Lake), worked as translation consultant for Zhongkun Cultural Fund, Beijing, and served as translator for Jidi Majia (Deputy Chair, Chinese Writers Association). Denis translated books by the Buddhist monk Shih Chen-hua (SUNY Albany, 1992), the philosopher Feng Youlan (Hawaii University, 2000), and the art critic Zhu Zhu (Hunan Fine Arts, 2009). His poetry translations include: *Frontier Taiwan* (Columbia University Press, 2005); *Contemporary Chinese Poetry* (Shanghai Literary Arts, 2007); Yan Zhi, *Reading the Times* (Homa & Sekey, 2012); Jidi Majia, *Rhapsody in Black* (Univ. of Oklahoma, 2014); Jidi Majia, *Shade of Our Mountain Range* (Mkhiva Foundation, 2014); Luo Ying, *Memories of the Cultural Revolution* (Univ. of Oklahoma, 2015); Jidi Majia, *From the Snow Leopard to Mayakovsky* (Kallatumba Press, 2017); Yang Ke, *Two Halves of the World Apple* (Univ. of Oklahoma, 2017), as well as *7+2 Mountain Climber's Journal* (White Pine, 2020). He has also translated poetry by Yan Li, Meng Lang and many others. His own poetry collection *Man Cut in Wood* was published by Valley Contemporary Poets (Los Angeles, 2004).

PREFACE

By Yan Li

The spirit of poetry has consistently been an aspect of civilization. Two kinds of good poetry are possible, namely the poetry of written words and the poetry of behavior, of which the latter is more important. Why? Because the former is derived from the latter. A number of poets may feel that behaving poetically is difficult, so they choose the former in isolation from the former, but this would leave them with nothing but written technique.

With reference to Chinese poetry, in order to make its influence felt internationally, it must grow out of a capacity for poetic action that is expressed through cultural behavior. In a period when human beings are facing existential crises, does our spiritual orientation have attainments to offer? Of course we can point to certain prize winning literary and cinematic works. Yet the poetic spirit is not a matter of national or international recognition. It lies in whether or not a modern individual really undertakes to pass on the heart of poetry. I believe there can be no poetry without reflection. Only by reflecting on personal behavior, national behavior, disastrous events and uncivilized incidents can one develop and pass down the poetic spirit. What is more, there is no hand in this world that can't engage in some form of handiwork, there is only a distinction between whether one engages or not. Thus poets have a habit of taking time to reflect on things before choosing what is worth engaging in: we often describe this as "availing oneself of something according to the Way." The word "Way" in this expression is the Way of moral striving. Considered from another angle, an individual's writing is always free, regardless of whether his attempts to be published meet with adverse or favorable circumstances. So whether there are chances to be published or not, when one has authentic feelings it is good to write them down and see what happens. Only in this way is there a possibility that greater numbers of authentic works can be preserved and handed down.

This anthology of poems in English translation was prepared by the American poet/ sinologist Denis Mair. It gathers poems written by Chinese-speaking poets who came to America at various times over the past 40 years. It focuses on poets who have lived under different social systems and reveals their thoughts as they grapple with matters of immigrant psychology, identity and homesickness. This body of work has been compiled into an English-language volume, in hopes that American readers can get an idea of how Chinese emigré poets approach and articulate their experiences of modern life......

Finally I would like to say that poetry translation can help expand the shared space of international literature. Thanks to the translator Denis Mair! Thanks to the Iris & Junming Le Foundation for sponsoring the publication of this volume.

April 2025 (National Poetry Month)

Table of Contents

Hanshan Laoteng

寒山老藤

Hanshan Laoteng is a Chinese-speaking poet living in Brooklyn, New York. His works are distributed in electronic publications and paper media. "In the writing of poetry, I try to use the concise and implicit techniques from the Chinese poetry tradition to express the thinking about human nature in Western literature."

BEHIND A WINDOW

Their souls are on the other side
of those fleshly envelopes
Their coffee—along with joy, anger and sorrow—
are on the other side of glass
I stand behind a window, watching the street
as if the fall wind only withers the passers-by

Behind a window, like a clay jug
left and forgotten
nobody knowing that I exist   and then
nobody knowing that I don't exist
as if the passers-by are in a script
only one's soul can draw near to them

Nov. 2023

SNOW

Already in late fall, my visions of snowy scenes
were in their final draft
When the snow would fall
was not up to me

and it wasn't not up to the snow either
Snow's meaning is not just to highlight
a line of footprints that guide the way ahead
but sometimes that's what they must do

especially after forcing maple leaves to withdraw,
with their color that was all the rage for a time
setting winter's stage for a unanimous yes to snow
achieving something in a cause of conscience

Once spring warmth brings flowers, the snow
must give way, leaving its sullied name on the land
Fate is apportioned to everyone
victory or defeat is not up to oneself

Nov. 26, 2023

MINIMAL

Having been through a gust of Kandinsky's wind
lines and colors come alive in imagination
Unbearable happenings and dark times are brought
by imagination's guidance to philosophy's door

A minimalist, looking for things to do, has deleted
the plot points of rain that poured down on the city
It falls from the sky over roofs and into ditches
dirtied by where it flows before entering the sea

Just as I, before I entered into worldly matters
which changed me in ways I couldn't expect
was my pared-down self, with nothing to hide
a naked human life, not a subject for abstraction

Oct. 21, 2023

Yi Chu

一初

Yi Chu's ancestral home was Yueyang, Hunan, and she lives in a small village in South Dakota. She published an English poetry collection *Ordinary Heart.* In her early years, she published poems and prose in *Guangzhou Daily, Micro Literature,* and *Dongting Literary Magazine.* Good at oil painting, life aesthetics, poetry, prose, and novels. "I like to write about nature and countryside, as well as life experiences and love poems, and follow the principle of simplicity."

PASSING BY

Passing through a clump of grass
a leaping grasshopper makes way for you

A cloud meets another cloud
sounds of wind filling a pine grove
grow hushed in their encampment

At this moment she is the one
abiding with the seclusion of a flower

So-called love that once stirred the soul
flowed elsewhere like water in a riverbed

The riverbed holds only chunks of deadwood
and its gravel hides the spray of waves

This is a river without a name
like her having passed through his life
now nowhere to be found

LOWLY LOVE

I'm a cloud bearing the rain as fruit
When you stand by a row of plantain trees
I fall upon your shoulders
and look at you wetly

I am a buoyant gust of morning wind
at the moment that you turn about
I lightly brush the corner of your eye

I am the pond's water, swollen in autumn
When you lower your head towards me
many swords seem to pierce my chest
These waters are stirred to restlessness
and grief that comes in eddies

SUPPOSE THAT...

Suppose that love were a contrafactual assumption
I would join you to tread upon fire without hesitation
even if it meant tempering my body to metal

I have come bringing a shovel and snowflakes as seeds
with my withering and rootlessness from many lifetimes

Leave the lintel of springtime's door
for my moonlight to wax and wane upon

A fish without wings
finds a place for itself in the water

I will be buried in your mountain range
to be nourished by your love that stretches far

One who comes from the Yangtze
will pass by again and again

Always showing graceful restraint
always enduring minor sorrows

Zora

左拉

Zora, whose real name is Wan Yingling, holds a master's degree in public administration and is an executive of American technology and medical institutions. She has studied painting since childhood and loves writing. Her works have been published in periodicals such as *First Line New York*, *Slave Society*, and *Houston Poetry Garden*. She is the author of the poetry and painting collection *The Journey of No Confusion* and the illustrated book *Eye of the Dragon*. More information about the author and work can be found at zorawanart.com

LOCK

A stone without a shape
presses upon my stomach
like the crease between your brows…

Downward arcs of the lip corners
which have locked up your former smile
are pressed in seriousness

It is making demands of you:
"Give me your time
Give me your concentration
Give me your flesh
Give me
Give it all"

Your soul is tightly locked
within your fleshly envelope
A gigantic invisible hand
pulling the leash
yanks you along

No room to negotiate
no leeway given
no interstice
demanding the entirety of flesh
to set multi-ton machinery in motion

This commences from the top down
whereupon the leash pauses to watch
and you catch a moment's breath

It turns about
tightens the leash
continues

You are left there
by yourself
in a far spot
Sobbing

THE RIVER OF PASSING TIME

The river of time flows over our bodies
leaving rolling hills or maybe canyons
The river of time flows over our faces
a placid lake may turn into a desert
The river of time flows over our hearts
burying love in silence

The river of time slows to a trickle
the past is never really past
it only remains upstream
too hard to trace, too far to touch
but it is there in the moment two hands touch
it opens a window
when eyes meet eyes

The river of time slows to a trickle
The future has already happened
even though the happening is downstream
Darkness and light may be hard to know
but their marks are drawn in a palmprint
Their wishes are buried in hearts
like the pole star guiding our course

The river of time slows to a trickle
a moment of full immersion in the flow
comes riding a white horse onto the scene

There is nowhere to hide oneself away
The only way is to breathe together with it
to throw open the organs of perception
to plunge into the cosmos head on
to flow where the waves take you

Everything ends up in stillness
The river of time slows to a trickle

SPRINGTIME IS CRYING

Springtime leans against the roof and cries
that blustery stir rouses the one
who was just climbing out of a dream
Its wailing cries dispel a long winter's gloom
bringing release from pent-up days in a California forest

Spring's sobs rub against the winter
its constant drizzling tears
keep a sunlight-loving heart
imprisoned inside a house, as if
to carry out a ceremonial offering
That which is offered will be
a smile that only remained in memory
a silhouette that receded into darkness
a span of sunny days that can't be recovered

Sobbing spring hugs a gold-haired, red-lipped wife
Who wouldn't want to grow old together, children all around?
Why did you let that one go, to be snared in fate's trap alone?
The world always lines up in symmetries
A sensitive heart can always make a choice
For any amount of selfishness, there is also
the same amount of uprightness
Darkness and light share the same heart

Springtime covers its face and weeps
shedding tears for one who bravely strode into fire
grieving for one who was pulled into desire's black hole

Springtime cries out loud, to cleanse them all
those hotly churning hearts all over the world

March 2024

Land Fish

陆地鱼

Land Fish, whose real name is Xiao Ying, was born in Beijing and raised in Anhui; holds a Doctorate in Engineering. Now living in Seattle, USA, working in the energy industry. She loves words, and her poetry won first prize at the first New York Flushing Poetry Festival in 2018.

AT THE BEACH WITH MY SON
ON JULY 4TH

At the sky's edge, July's blue drumbeats advance grandly
summoning youthful surfers on wings of foam
Your shirt bellies out like a pristine conch shell
eager for the wind to sound its trumpet

I know someday you'll become an outlander
just as I did many years ago
this is doubtlessly ordained by destiny
as if on the wheel of reincarnation

The world is so huge, I cannot imagine
how many stars will pave the way for your feet
how many islets you will raise out of storms
how many windows you'll open to gaze afar

At each moorage, if only you look back and wave
a wind will whirl back to brush my face
—just as one is whirling now

to those who face the wind with teary eyes
I love all of you

July 4, 2018

SNOWFALL IS A TIME OF REDEMPTION*

At daybreak sunlight shines through me from behind
and in the evening likewise. Between the two times
the sky is totally open to the light, looking down on
the withering and falling of gold leaves

Some of them fall towards your sleeping forehead
the wind tugging them is about to rush this way, but you
are farther away than the water from which the cosmos was born
I cannot even touch it with the scent of a tangerine

Like the butterfly this fall, from the southern hemisphere
it was actual, as was its uneasy heartbeat
Even more actual is a swelling volcano on the seafloor
and the suffocation of time by amusements

What was prophesied will emerge like rocks in a riverbed
as we go about our business, not really noticing

I go barefoot, proceeding on foot amid flames
No sooner do you speak of snow, than it starts falling
Snowflakes are wings, born in the moment a bell starts tolling
Snow is redemption; snow is forgetting after many years

Nov. 12, 2017

*In Chinese, the image of snow can be used as a metaphor for redress or vindication. (Tr)

IN SPRINGTIME

The whole world is blooming
(perhaps only by virtue of flowers
is the coming of spring beyond a doubt)
I've found that I am growing thorns
compassion and fury alike have sharp edges

—I look forward to growing even more thorns
I also look forward to everyone growing thorns, because
in this human world full of lurking things, thorns are needed
just as a strong spine and salt and light are needed

I've put forth too many delicate blooms
Before I end up reaching my ultimate cessation
I need to let all the thorns grow on me
that should have been growing on me

To let memories of Sodom's sins fade would be shameful
A world that only lets flowers bloom is more shameful

As for those who grow thorns
and are bloodied by sharp thorns
they will ultimately die, yet ultimately
they will grow wings of redemption

March 4, 2020

Yang Hao

杨皓

Yang Hao, Chinese-American poet, art critic, curator, art collector, founder and director of the Murray Hill Art Museum in New York, chairman of the American Chinese Contemporary Art Foundation, Top 100 Collectors Group Chairman. He is the author of the poetry collection *Crossing the River and Burning the Bridge* (Writers Press), and the art criticism collection *The Journey of Adventures* (Peking University Press).

I AM UP IN HEAVEN WATCHING YOU

I am up in heaven watching you
your long hair and your waist
I watch you run on a beach
as the wind blows your sighs away
I am watching you
as time pursues you
I watch your white skirt
tossed in the wind

I am up in heaven watching you
watching your loneliness
your travels between ocean and dry land
the emptiness of your heart
and the smiles you wear on your face
I watch your dignity
being summoned forth by the wind
by which I can read
the extent of your loneliness

I am up in heaven watching you
my beloved beauty
leaning beside a bed of fragrant herbs
Passing years enhance your dreams
but they do away with your smile
I see that even your tears

are being transformed
to incense ash

I am up in heaven watching you
watching the wild winds blowing
against your image in a mirror
and the waves they stir
in your empty heart
watching your long-suffering search
watching you in solitude
with nothing to rely on

A LONE CLOUD OVER NEW YORK

A lone cloud over New York
has a lone star
hiding behind it
Solitary and coldly aloof
with a mysterious smile
peering down on the city

She surveys New York through the glass
of a hundred thousand light years
Gazing down with deep feeling
at humankind's uncanny laboratory
the thought of her own star system
totally slips her mind

From a reflection in a drop of water
and from deep in an infant's eye
I catch sight of that lone star
behind that lone cloud

A LETTER TO VAN GOGH

Van Gogh
Ever since I said farewell
to you in Arles
a deeper melancholy
has come over me
In reply to your question
I too have been admitted
to a mental health ward
except that the facilities here
are fancier than yours
I went to your wheat fields
but the flock of crows did not return
The waists of sunflowers
were even more hunched
The olive groves where you lingered
on the hills at Saint-Rémy,
are producing less than ever
Many of their branches
are unwilling to bear fruit
due to outrage at this world
Beneath the Langlois Drawbridge
I saw dead fish floating
Outside of the hotel where we had coffee
there was a young man
in the throes of anomie

Van Gogh

when will you go with me to China

There are many copies of your biography there

you gaze distractedly from the covers

some are growing mold in the dampness

The rainy season there

may aggravate your condition

Wouldn't it be better

not to be so angry at Gaugin?

If he wants to go to Tahiti

let him go, even if

he continues on from there

to Martinique as well

We can go to Wuhan together

then to Beijing and Shanghai

Van Gogh

After you and I

said goodbye at Arles

you have never left me

My condition

is also getting serious

I hope you'll be patient

and let me get through

this rainy season

Shuangyi

双一

Shuangyi, whose real name is Yang Jinghai, lives in Hawaii and is the author of the poetry collection *People Walking on the Earth*. His works have appeared in various poetry magazines such as *First Line New York, Genesis, New World, Chinese Poetry, International Poetry*, and have been included in various poetry anthologies and yearbooks. He has won the first prize at the New York Flushing Poetry Festival, as well as the Sino Literature Award and the Global Chinese Poetry Award.

CONTAINER

Before coming into this world
a child is a puff of cloud
Down here on earth the child begins
by becoming a rill of pellucid water

Making its way through the world's twists and turns
It must learn inclusiveness
Amid grains of sand and dust it finds
a container of one color or another
into which it carefully decants itself

As for me, I have used up half a lifetime learning
to place my container calmly and quietly
to receive the settling grains of sand and dust
Then the rest of this lifetime will be
devoted to breaking the container

ANSWER

This span of days, my belt has gotten looser.
Walking gets slower, steps trudge more heavily.
Cares and sorrows, these days, solidify to stones.
I'm a carrier of stones

we are all carriers of stones.
Headstones in the graveyard are proof:
those stones on the shoulder at last unloaded
placed in front of a body lying flat

My hunched reflection is suspended
on the lake's surface; fish swishing their tails
pass through it; I want to exchange bodies with a fish
and glide through water as if in free fall

I'm on the bank watching fish
Does the sky have a pair of eyes to watch me?

"My yoke is easy, and my burden is light."
This is the answer the sky gives. It has been wanting
to trade bodies with me, but I don't understand
just as fish don't understand why I hunch my spine

REFRAIN

The days are stirred by the vast sea into troughs and crests
We are notes upon those undulating curves
On time's lingering violin string, between bursts of sound
and rests, all the pauses and syncopation
the diminuendos and crescendos
are what comprise us
We put up castle walls on a sand beach
We mark our direction with footprints
Our cries merge into the sea's seething allegro
and the bold ones who stake lives on steadfastness of wood
strike out from shore, charging into the open sea
until harvest-giving waves push them back onto shore
to and fro they go; the finger of purpose traces out a rhythm
We lean towards the red sun that sets in the sea's blue cradle
at night, and the ocean strokes violin strings with its breath
Some wakeful notes stare darkness in the face
Some notes slump their heads and fall asleep

A POEM OF SILENCE

This time, the Gulag Archipelago imprisons words
for crimes committed against blank paper and screens

Words that escape the lips disappear in the wind
Those caught by the fingers submit themselves to the net

Fruits fallen into a basket, starlight gathered into eyes
The resting place of honesty in words is a high wall

Those gyrating on a public stage get sore in the waist and knees
Those flouncing about in negligees are bound for a mental ward

If I come to know nature's goodness by fruit and starlight
then from words I learn to write poems of silence

Yes, silence. On the charnel hill of words there are few
gravestones
and even if there are, the inscriptions are mostly effaced

I bury my poems in the ground there
I want my words to make silent thunder

Xinye Qiu

邱辛晔

Known as Paul by his colleagues and friends, Xinye was born in 1962. After studying in the Chinese Department of Fudan University in the 1980s, Paul worked at Shanghai Joint Publishing. In 1990, he went to New York to study and later worked at the Queens Library. He served as Assistant Library Manager of the Flushing Library for over twenty years. He has written, translated and edited many books. Since 2018, he has served as an Executive Director of the Flushing Poetry Festival in New York.

THAT CITY

The windshield keeps wind outside
the tree chooses to stay where it is
planted to endure guard duty at a gravestone
He who comes to pay awkward respects still seeks
the optimum rhetoric to express his feelings

Having been lined up in tidy rows
the residents of this city
endorse what the United Nations should be
Jews, blacks, whites, Chinese
all came with their own stories
There is no Secretary-General
there is no Property Management Association
no fracas over who will be given the floor next
The stutterers and the loquacious ones
are equally silent, and passing years
have assimilated them to one skin color
As for the languages on their gravestones
and which religions are embraced
that is a matter for graveside visitors

THE CRUCIAL PARTS OF A LIVING THING

The breasts of a woman
swell with the might of a great river
that bestows nourishment on either bank
 The womb of a woman erects the walls
of the first cozy nest in a person's life
As for a man, the torrential sperm
delivered by his prostate is comparable
to the parting and meeting of Red Sea waters

And yet, the crucial parts of a living thing
often lead to a distorted, freakish denouement
stirring up a latent climax of a different kind
outside of the script instilled in men and women
where they cannot fathom what should be written

March-April, 2024

OCEAN

One expanse of ocean is the brother of all oceans
but the planet insists on maintaining its innate rotation
and so there is never a billow
that fully submits to another billow
Waves crash against other waves
in the Black Sea
the Arabian Sea
the South China Sea and the Baltic Sea
three meter waves overlook all the rest
wildly shooting spray from their tips

Crest after crest like white flowers
as they smash and break into spume
In this grim civil war they sacrifice themselves
for the sake of peaceful, low undulations
they once enjoyed in common

April 2023

A GUIDE TO WINE TASTING

Having been sealed off for over a month
the carnation could only unleash itself
in Shanghai's inner life
The neighborhood associations said
no matter how hidden, it must be given up
to the guards in white suits, but my take on this
sees a key to tasting newly offered wines:
The white of 2022 will ferment into a vintage
that won't fall short of the red of 1966 *

May 2022

*Note ∶ The color white is associated with the hazmat suits of
sanitation enforcers during the Covid-19 pandemic. White was also
associated with blank signs that demonstrators held up during street
marches against compulsory lockdowns in some Chinese cities during
2022. (Tr.)*

Heifeng

黑丰

Hei Feng, poet, writer. Works: poetry collections *Empty Pregnancy, Above the Ashes, Two Nights of the Cat, The Deep Passage of Time,* etc.; experimental novel collection *Butterflies Are Half of the Afternoon*; essay collections *The Bottom of Everything* and *Existence-Flicker.* Awards: Special Honor Award at the Arges International Poetry Festival in Romania, Historic Capital Poet Award at the 6th International Poetry Festival in Iasi; ASA University New York International Culture and Arts Festival Contribution Award, New York Flushing Poetry Festival Chinese Poetry Translation Award. He is a judge and final judge for important awards such as the 4th China Young Chinese Writers Award and the Beijing White Bird Award.

SMASHED CUCUMBER

— Thoughts of An Overseas Chinese

—A cucumber can be minced in many ways
simply by smashing it with the flat of a knife

A cook can smash a cuke to look like a stillborn infant
or smash it so it won't want to be reborn as a cucumber
With a smack that could turn a person into a brain-dead cuke
a cuke can be smashed so that it resembles a moribund culture
A nationality on the block can be smashed to look like a mushy
cuke
A man's balls and masculinity and spine can be smashed away
his inborn conscience can be smashed out of him
A woman's motherliness and femininity can be smashed away
so that she barely looks female and human

Father in heaven, my pity will never let me smash so precisely
my smacking technique will always fall short of our national
heritage

Shaped like a gall bladder, with pointy bumps and a flower stub
a cucumber is such a tender, diminutive thing

You bear down on it with tempestuous movements
like the dark clouds of a cyclone

You really don't need to overpower it so mightily

no need to be so thunderous…what stormy force possesses
you?

Your way of smacking down sends juice and gobbets flying
it scatters the wits, makes the soul lose its bearings

An earthquake comes to Times Square in Manhattan
the Hudson River floods and flows
   backward
The impact is felt on China's Yangtze River
all the ships go off course; signal lights are knocked out…

Just a little cucumber, along with people at the scene
like exquisite jade reduced to fragments by your hand
a nationality with its cultural possibilities, gone to pieces
on the chopping block of Manhattan, in pieces
dregs to be cast off in a black garbage bin
by casting off others you cast yourself away
human dregs only fit for a cremation urn

My poetry-writing pen keeps trembling
the Goddess of Liberty's hand is also trembling

Do you deserve to be called a woman?
Do you deserve to be called a person?

Those things you smash with the flat of your knife
things you are smacking with such vehemence…
are they fit for people to eat? Are they edible?

You use a murderous heart to smash cucumbers
you use cucumber-smashing strokes to kill people

Your abilities and attainments, such as they are
are only fit for the rear kitchen of that iron house in China
not for getting in the faces of countrymen new to the USA
(try smacking a python or crocodile and see what happens)

Today, I need to spit out this phlegm stuck in my throat
to spit you out, revolted by the sliminess I'm hawking up
It will take lifetimes of effort, and as I press the toilet knob
I thoroughly flush you into the New York night
all the way to the dark sewers of China

DON'T

You can add a bitter teardrop
add a bit of salt; you can even
add oil drained from a kitchen gutter

Just don't let the votive lamp
get too empty
don't let the flame
start guttering too much
don't let the Buddha feel too forlorn

Aug. 2018

A SOLITARY NAIL

Every single nail here
was pounded in by her, all alone

Each nail was driven in helplessness
Each nail was driven in valor

Each nail is the nail of one person only
Each nail is the nail of one who sheds blood

To build takes loss of blood, to build a woman's dwelling
to build a heart's nest for dreams, to be done with drifting

Jan. 22, 2023 in New York

Su-la

苏拉

Su-la, poet, now lives in New Jersey. Poems have been published in *New World, First Line New York, Poetry Magazine, Survivor*, etc. Recommended poet of the year by the Poetry Island website in 2022. Author of poetry collection *Flowers of Other Worlds.*

BUTTERFLY

Do not be afraid to become infinite
do not use words to repair your life

Do not say "beauty this" or "beauty that"

Beauty is always a completely new world
that lights up every grain of dust
Whatever you possess will turn around
and possess you in turn

For no reason go and love
like a flower in the wind
opening layer by layer

Like a shadow, follow the sun
in one interval find a thousand sunsets
You call what is oceanic a butterfly
Ah stranger, where will you take me?

I WANT TO LIVE WITHIN FLAMES

I want to live within flames, with a ring
of flame on my finger, in a room of flame;
within books of flame there is
a print font with no straight lines.
Half will be body, and half
the melted currency of soul,
neither on the side of life nor death.
Each kind of medicine creates a new sickness,
and higher tongues of flame pounce forth
each time I am gazed at. A stark naked yogi
bears the harsh chill on a snowy peak
resisting the contradictions of desire.
But I will immerse myself in flame
following her emotive dance steps. A secret
that wins transcendence leaves you no choice

SOLAR ECLIPSE

Mexicans once taught me
to observe the sun through obsidian lenses.
Hundreds of millions of solar plasma cells erupt
in high-velocity ejections of coronal mass,
shining through black glass as a soft annular ring,
a smudgy yellow illusion.

Am I also a dream? Has a dazzling god
dreamt me into existence over the past thousand years?
Awakening, like the eclipsed sun re-emerging
I am murmuring
as I become whole again.

Yunzhong-que

云中雀

Yunzhong-que, whose real name is Jason Xu, is a member of the Los Angeles Chinese Writers Association and the first prize winner of the first New York Flushing Poetry Festival; 2020 *Mei Pian Best Judges' Award*. Won first prize in the Southern California Poetry Competition in 2021. His works were published in *Reader* and *Yangtze River Poetry. LA Poetry Magazine, First Line New York* , *China Press* and *World Journal*, etc.

I LIKE THE LOOK OF YOU LYING ON YOUR SIDE

Outside the window, you are laid out
in geometrical lines
one leg stretched straight
one arched in a 90 degree angle
sturdy arms bent at 45 degree angles
setting my hormones raging

The sun highlights the high bridge of your nose
a sea of flowers tosses at your feet
wind spreads the sails of a poetry book
It would take a monarch butterfly
to make the pride of your knees submit

But this is what I like at this moment
the look of you lying on your side
assuming the outline of a suspension bridge
on which the figure of a woman dressed in purple
passes over the giant cello of your body

IMPRESSIONS ON A RIVERBANK

After so many years
a horse carries me back
its zebra-like reflection striped by ripples
amid purling of water, I say nothing
the horse, too, says nothing

In the water, I am carrying the horse
adrift on a river of clouds
our feet are pointing skyward, where I see
the blue sky carrying white clouds
and they too say nothing.

Wang Jiaxin

王家新

Wang Jiaxin, poet, critic, and translator, was born in Danjiangkou City, Hubei Province in 1957. After graduating from high school, he was transferred to the labor force. After the "Cultural Revolution", he was admitted to the Chinese Department of Wuhan University. In 2006, he was appointed as a professor by the School of Liberal Arts of Renmin University of China (now retired). He has authored 40 to 50 collections of poems, poetry essays and translated poems, including the German poetry anthology *Poems of Late Arrival*, the English poetry anthology *Darkening Mirror*, the Croatian poetry anthology *Night Train*, His Dutch poetry anthology *Ashes of Dawn* and other works have won various domestic and foreign poetry awards, poetic criticism awards and translation awards. In recent years, he has lived in New York and was invited to be a writer-in-residence in Amsterdam. He has lectured and recited at some universities, literary festivals, literary centers and libraries in the United States and Canada.

YEARS OF HUNGER

Back then my family didn't starve like nearby villagers
my parents taught in the middle and primary schools

My mother got hold of an old hen somewhere
but one day when she came home from teaching

She found the floor strewn with drumsticks and wings
half-cooked and unchewable

She gave me a thrashing, and the cries I made
brought all the neighbors to look in the doorway
—this story was told to me in adolescence
I was four years old at the time, maybe five

I don't remember any of it, but I know
that little boy is still crying

I also know that each weak sob
almost dies in his throat, yet he still cries

And amid those sobs that reach so far, I am writing
I know that behind those sobs, there are still more sobs

I know no memorial has been erected on this land
that would move us to bow before it

Thus I write, I am writing amid sobbing sounds
that reach me even now, I keep writing

May 2024

INTO THE BOSTON SUBWAY, FOR HA JIN

A headful of white hair, doubly dyed by frosts
of New England and China's Northeast
radiantly glows from a dim corner
of the Harvard Faculty Club

Dressed like Wu Nan,* a character
in your own novel, who wore an old sport coat to class
not having time to change after work

You led me out, with that eager look from thirty years ago
around the corner from the back of Harvard Bookstore
to a bookstore specializing in poetry
Then we spoke parting words; my eyes followed you
as you disappeared into the entrance of the Boston subway
Once again, after all those years, you reminded me
of the opening passages of Dante's Divine Comedy**

*Note: Wu Nan is the name of the lead character in Ha Jin's novel, A Free Life. The book tells of a former graduate student who becomes a restaurant owner and raises a family in America.

**Note: In the opening passage of Dante's Divine Comedy, the narrator meets the poet Virgil, who becomes his guide and escorts him to explore the underworld. (Tr.)

ON A FERRY RIDE

On the ferry from Staten Island to Manhattan
we pass by the Statue of Liberty

Some people lean on the railing taking photos
some sit on deck chairs basking in sunlight

She still holds her bronze torch high
but you no longer feel her breath as in past years

Once you reach America, "freedom" becomes a riddle
like the Bard's remark on rich men, who see vice in beggary*

The riddle prolongs that half-hour ferry trip
stretching it to an enactment of one's whole lifetime

It causes you to gaze at seagulls chasing each other
vying to be first to find what turns up in the boat's wake

March 2024

Note: Shakespeare wrote, "Whiles I am a beggar, I will rail and say there is no sin but to be rich; and being rich, my virtue then shall be to say there is no vice but beggary." (King John, Act.2, Scene 1) (Tr.)

TOTAL SOLAR ECLIPSE, APRIL 8, 2024

From Mexico City to Washington D.C. to Montreal, it's coming
to the aching pupils of the Northern Hemisphere
the amazing spectacle of the North American solar eclipse
It's like a line I read once by the Sichuan poet Ya Shi:
"a gravestone comes skimming along the ground"

April 8, 2024

Li Xiaohong

李笑虹

Li Xiaohong is the director of the Cellular Neurobiology Laboratory at the New York State Institute for Basic Research. Her works have been published in various poetry journals at home and abroad and included in many poetry collections. In 2019, she was invited to hold a personal poetry recitation. She has won many awards for her poetry. She is the author of personal poetry collections *Rainbow, Arc of the Wind* and *Beyond All Colors*.

NINE FEMALE SOLDIERS FROM UKRAINE

I don't know how an old, ugly world
can be made worthy of such pretty, youthful smiles

Light drips down, hangs there in the stillness
a snowy bright glance in the darkness
slicing through the fleshly envelope of darkness

Nine, then six, and then four
no, it is nine
between this shore and the further shore
from deathly quiet to keening that ignites a flame

In the sky is a bullet hole that sheds tears
raindrops grow wings
someone uses her shapely body
to fill up the shell of a word's meaning

SUNSET

Catch a shot of that certain instant
if there is such beauty
if the inexorable sky presses the water surface

Rose color will no longer disappear
rose-colored things will not disappear

So why don't you
take the half of you that remains
and place it in the sunset
Page through a dozen days
while your feet do not cross the threshold

A graded ink wash laid on, folds of translucency, with light
Inextricable from shadows, and a secret clenched in the hand

The sky says, my love bears down grandly over vast acres
the water says, my heavens, I have only a single drop

WILDFLOWER

Such is the way I blossom ceaselessly
Like gathering sunlight, I gather your every gaze
You know how hard I try

I am not one of those blossoms that are readily picked
I am here, beside a stream, at the corner of a wall
a diminutive spot of color, perhaps pale
perhaps vivid, a springtime dabbing of color
that by wishfulness you try to dash off at one go

The day will come, I will disappear
overnight without the slightest struggle
but I won't let you see my tearful countenance
My painful wound is forever hidden
behind the bright color blooming

BENEATH THE SETTING SUN

This loveliness seems to creep up
by means of its batik-like pattern of warm words
used to describe every living thing
including the sketchy and solitary ones
those suffering wounds of the soul
or even those withered-away ones

precisely because the moments are so fleeting
the look of one who bows at the waist
gives a sense of motherliness

BLANKNESS – AN AUTISTIC DIARY

It was the snow that emptied out time, and you
are no longer found in the words of my copious verse
comparable to a storm of virtual whiteness
that icy fluff which gives way to a mere puff or a flick—
wasn't it my way of coaxing you open?

A mirror has broken into countless pieces
I can find you in every one of them

As I wrap the mirage of a tree in my embrace
night's darkness seems of long acquaintance
someone once retrieved word-nuggets from stars there
A lingering leaf still twists on a branch tip
a tad lighter than the fullness of hope

I know, it isn't the wind
but a patch of blankness
that prompted me to claw in the snow
leaving those long marks

Bing guo

冰果

Bing guo is a co-editor of *First Line NewYork*. Her works are scattered in publications such as *Genesis* and *Hong Kong Literature*. Many of her works are included in joint collections such as *New York Streaming Poems and Shadows, Shout* and *Keep Dashing Madly on the Road of Reflection*.

SPRINGTIME

I fear the sound of firecrackers
I fear that long series of staccato blasts
And the sound of cardboard tubes splitting apart in mid-air
Which jolts all creatures out of their sweet slumber

In springtime they should wake up naturally
Once the spring season is here
The right day and hour will eventually come
In a perfectly natural way
They will open their eyes

MISTAKES

I have made mistakes
for which I'm not looking to be forgiven

In a clump of trees by a lake I'll dig a hole
One by one I'll admit my regrets
for each one I'll drop in a hard-shelled nut

Squirrels that run out of food can dig them up
So to some extent there will be good intentions
that will be linked to those mistakes I made.

Feb. 10, 2018

BESIDE A GLACIAL LAKE IN OAKLAND

When new growth thrusts itself upward
Striving to emerge from caked mud
It resembles a determined impulse of the heart

Some tender sprouts give up their lives
Beaten down by unexpected snowstorms

Those remaining, being a bit more lucky,
Find openings between decayed leaves
And appear like rivulets of green
That trickle out from a spring

Before I can get myself ready
My heart is already engulfed

Chen Minghhua

陳銘華

Chen Minghhua, whose ancestors hail from Fanyu, Guangdong Province, was born Dec. 1956 in Gia Dinh, Vietnam. In Dec. 1990 he co-founded *New World Poetry Monthly* and has served as its editor-in-chief ever since. His published collections include *Biography of a River* (poems) and *Ladder to Heaven* (prose poems).

HOLLOW

Clouds are writhing; the West Wall is writhing; al-Buraq Wall is writhing; eyes, ears, mouth, nose, skull, chest cavity… each opening more vacuous than the last, as the wall goes wriggling towards the southwest

One millennium passes and then another; still the openings in the Wall gape wider, shedding blood and tears

Feb. 10, 2024

TREE GHOST

Over the weekend in a corner of the garage I stumbled upon a trunkful of locked-up souls. Having been sealed up in a plastic sheet, their 11 x 8.5" bodies were still glossy! These must have been my old paramours, because I totally forgot them after my newly beloved DOS computer appeared.

Right now they are watching me silently and mournfully, their glances beseeching me so helplessly, that it takes me back to a road through forest shades, where my companions once gathered for an excursion. Maybe next spring new growth can still sprout from their branch tips.

Dec. 3, 2022

ABSURDIST THEATER PIECE 10

In cherry blossom season, shreds of secret documents bloom
against the backdrop of D.C.'s sky, with dryads peering through
the cracks between— the glances of people wishing to have an
erection once again.

April 21, 2023

Joan Xie

谢炯

Joan Xie is a lawyer and a prolific writer of poetry and essays, both in English and Chinese, as well as a poem translator. Xie's poetry and essay collections include *Half-Century Journey* (2015), *Looking Back* (2016), *Nothing Made Me Happier than Finding These Objects* (2018). In 2017, she received Second Prize at First Moganshan International Poetry Festival in China. Her poems in Chinese appeared in prestigious poetry magazines such as *Poetry Journal (Shikan)*, *The Yangtze River Poetry Journal* and *Peach Blossom Poetry* in China. Her poems in English and translations are published at *Exchanges Literature Journal*, *Lips* and *Poetry Sky* in the United States.

HALF A LIFETIME'S JOURNEY

All shapes and sizes of who you are
go into making the footsteps of life

You wear a pair of high heeled shoes
in a wild dance beneath a crystal chandelier
your emotions are ever-changing
a series of phantoms and impish notions
at times wearing a snow-white mask
or donning a cape won in a Faustian bargain

You wear a pair of snow boots
tramping through new snow over pine needles
or across the frozen surface of Lake George
falling countless times, getting to your feet again
for the tender warmth in a barely visible cabin

You wear a pair of running shoes
walking down the roads
of this mundane realm
A floral dress flounces in bright sunlight
bells hasten you into timeless dusk
You do not check a map or ask the way
any street or lane you choose is your destination

You wear a pair of flip-flops
on a beach in summer

treading light or heavy footprints by turns
at times pausing, enticed by a pink nautilus shell
at times giving in to the sea's azure flirtations
As the tide rises and falls,
gulls that can't bear aloneness wheel overhead

You once thought of readying a pair
of shoes embroidered with folk designs
which you would wear
either to enter heaven or hell

You once felt nostalgic for the pair
of klutzy Orphan Annie shoes
that Mother made you wear to school

The journey of half a lifetime
was always carried on in the moment
Your only wish was to go home
to take off your shoes in the dark
and occupy a quiet place at a window
Then you would pour yourself a glass
to taste intoxicating solitude until dawn

GOING FAR AWAY

Are you too among the insignificant:
all the buds, petals, and seeds
that taken together comprise a tree?
Have you also been informed
That you exist for the sake of that tree?
Well then, if you end up falling
How far from the tree can it take you?
Now I sit among all of you
Actively seeking a magpie hungry enough
To have an exchange of wings with me

NESTING RUSSIAN DOLLS

The year I turned six
I was hospitalized for illness
My release was on China-Russia Friendship Day
The director came through the wards
and gave a present to each little patient
a set of nesting Russian dolls
The sky was very blue that day
the lake was aquamarine
Willows made a wispy line
like palace ladies on an opera stage
I lay in a quilt on a pedicab
as my father pedaled up a long slope
Letting out a few dry coughs
and turned to look at me

I dozed with lowered eyelids
but held the dolls under the quilt
opening them one by one
each wore a colorful babushka
their lovely eyes were big and round
their long upturned eyebrows
identically penciled
gave them a look of surprise
I opened them one by one
getting down to the smaller ones

getting closer to the true core
but the smallest, inmost one
could not be opened
It gave a rattling sound when shaken
Could there be an even smaller doll
locked up within the inmost one?
Reaching home; Father carried me inside

The nesting dolls were left forgotten
In the back of the borrowed pedicab
many years have gone by
but I still wonder
what withered smell was locked inside
that doll that couldn't be opened
It is just before 4 o'clock
streetlights are turning on
The Stars and Stripes flap quietly
on the flagpole above the bridgehead
A gust of wind sends leaves tumbling
along either side of the road
I walk to a ballfield under ragged clouds
and furtively take off my mask
After being stifled for so long
even the smell of withering is fragrant

COMING UPON A WILD PEAR TREE IN BLOOM

Behind a little post office in Bayonne Township
I came upon a wild pear tree in bloom
hunched over a green, unused mailbox
Her countenance was pale, with an uneasy look
like a fugitive from last lifetime's grave
Inhaling a whiff, I smelled
disinfectant from the underworld
and asked, "Why are you here?"...
which touched her sore spot; she looked stumped
unable to evade my metaphysical interrogation
Just then a Ford pulled in and changed direction
our nostrils caught the smell of hot steel
She seized the moment to smile sweetly
and kiss the palm of my hand
on which my life-line is getting shorter
Along the street, dwarf cherries reached out to grab
at the trailing skirts of cloud in drizzling rain

Da Wen

达文

Da Wen is from Taishan, Guangdong. Graduated from South China Institute of Technology, UCLA. Member of the Guangdong "Yuanliu" modern poetry group. He is currently an editorial board member of the New World Poetry Journal in Los Angeles and a member of Chinese writers in Los Angeles. His works have been published in "Yuanliu", "Yixing", "New World Poetry Magazine", "Works", "Poetic God", "Autumn Water", "World Daily", "International Daily", "Overseas Chinese News", and were included in "Yuyou" "Autumn Waters - Selected Poems for the 20th Anniversary of Autumn Waters", "The Century is Wandering - New Selected Chinese Poems in North America", "Centennial Poetry Selections", "Selected Chinese Poems in the 21st Century World" and other poetry anthologies. His creative experience was included in the "Dictionary of New Chinese Poetry from Taiwan, Hong Kong, Macao and Overseas". Published personal poetry collections as "Climate Window" (1993), "Fanfeng Port" (1994), "Sifang City" (1995 - a collection of four people).

GETTING FARTHER AWAY

You need not enter into the ocean
before you become concerned with boundaries

You need not drone on all afternoon
teasing out shadows of the air

You can assume there is a gathering of people
strangers to each other... seated in a row

You can assume a sunset as the background
for facing seagulls turning in a gyre

As they get farther away
you can imagine the spout of a whale

And that the instant of its exhalation
is more boundless than the fall of darkness

WAR HORSE— THE FILM THAT TOLD ITS STORY

At a time when tongues led a charge at the enemy
voices bloomed in treetops…
Racing sunlight flung shadows into the sky

Horseshoes were drumming the beat of a harvest
as the chord of machine gun fire swelled in a valley
The loftiest wingbeats crashed with the utmost fragility

Amidst onlooking roses
a man threw down his saber, just as his underlings
gave their bodies to be figures in a bas relief tableau

WINDMILL

Night and day we are a spectacle, content unto ourselves
On a smooth bed laid out in a grove of trees
Our lives are more nonchalant than any human's

What you call spaciousness
is your loss of sensitivity towards colors
You use books to set up prim and proper frontiers

Don Quixote, there is no need
For us to proceed towards a humdrum rendezvous
Put down your congenital lance!

Beyond the troupe of white shaggy-dog clouds
Set erect your hard-to-relinquish fantasies
Learn to whirl in martyrdom for a cause… to bathe in wind

Zhang Er

张耳

A native of Beijing, has lived on both sides of the United States for many years. She is the author of many collections of poetry, including "The Sea Jumps, Bullets Tactfully" published by Taipei Xiuwei in recent years, and "First Mountain" (First Mountain) by Zephyr Press in the United States. Mountain). Zhang Er is also engaged in editing overseas poetry magazines and poetry anthologies, and translating Chinese and English poetry. The works of American poet John Ashbery she translated have been published in "First Line New York", "Today", "Poetry Island", "Contemporary International Poetry" " and "World Literature" published. Her English operas Moon in the Mirror, Fiery Jade: Cai Yan and Tacoma Method, which she collaborated with American composers, have been performed in the United States in recent years.

THE COAST WHERE BIG WORDS EBB
AND FLOW

Chinese kungfu has come roaring onto the scene, just look:
those para-police stomping on Granny Shen's basket of oranges
what deft kicks and steady stances! But that's no big deal
For each day's mix of real and fake we compile codes, noting
down
our daily throes in the course of this sole lifetime, such as:

Those disgusting Mainland women who venture offshore
with their bodies carrying their only bargaining chips
for the sake of children, for the sake of a "coastal" style
feeling their way along… they manage to get a footing
Chinese mothers blush blood-red over this
shame dyes the East China Sea to a red tide
Gold-red coral, gold-red fireworks in early spring
are flaunted everywhere on this unromantic isle

On the coastline where big words ebb and flow
the wave pattern does not enlighten slavish minds
Disgusting Mainland women who venture to other shores
selling their only asset which they can control
other parts were dominated by schoolbooks and singsong
chants
their faces and thoughts were painted for them, reduced to
transparent wave caps on big data's bright pulsing sea.
Only the shame that remains within the mother's control,

can redeem a child's future, this spotless forehead
which still holds a promise of freedom, under her cupped hands.
Even if she breaks a stiletto heel, cannot pull on her shoe
waves of tears leave traces as she is trodden by the crowd
She feels her shell, her very bones being trod underfoot
reduced and strewn like golden sand by wanton waves

All grown distant. O Star Mother TOW MOO, for the slights
you've suffered, accept my bows and these apples, along with
my words of gratitude. As satin banners flap in the wind
don't mothers of China want to hold up their heads?
The rape of one Little Ruby is not new under the sun.
One line jotted by a Grand Marshall wipes out a forest redoubt.
Wind has not died down; a tiger howls, and the tiger slayer
has been forced into a hideout. What weight does refusal carry?
Even the serial rape of more than of 1.4 billion could happen.
Big words ebb and flow; little words fall like petals; children of
China

if they had balls wouldn't go over old ground.
walking back and forth
on the upper floor…in this life or the next, covert and overt plots,
campaigns, plans, paramilitaries, Public Security…
Oh children of China
Young Zhang, Little Red, Young Cui, Young Liu, Young Li alias
"little plum"
and Lackey Wang, maybe unable to pull on shoes, thus all the
more willing

to treat spilt blood as gold. Pining on spring's pillow in a hideaway
or earning food and shelter only to have an earthquake… perhaps
learning to rule or cure venereal disease by non-action.
The heart turns toward ocean regions, inky depth of night waters
a slumbrous bed broadening or shrinking, but on a greater scale…
Heaven may collapse, earth cave in… let waves of perception
tenderly model the world, and perhaps
after the sun rises, we too may summon up
a red-gold imprint of our sense of loss, diffusing its color
across the sky. We remember hoodlum-heroes
and where they went in February…[1] We use heaps of time
exchanging confidences in talk bars. On top of lies
and dreams, we have our modern decadence… Indeed
we spend our days in ways our parents wouldn't recognize…
days in a cage more crowded and thus perhaps oppressive

[1] *When Mainland China fell to the Communist Party in 1949,
Communist forces entered Wuhan and Beijing; both cities were sealed off
in February. It was a time of great upheaval and euphoria. Unfortunately,
while dealing with ideological enemies, the CCP did not proceed according
to due process. (Tr.)*

SONG OF THE FOUR SEASONS OF NOTHINGNESS

Procedural justice in the public interest, civil or criminal
like a sprig of new greenery, the key points marked by peach
blossoms
freedom's sundial shadow, variably short and long

Who cares? As for the distinction of blood and sweat
after soaking rain passes, all must be redone. Although blood
has no fingerprints, injustice trickles out just the same

In a cloudless fall wind, the idea of heaven
peeks over a wall; public opinion and para-police do face scans
Yellow poplar leaves rustle to the last page, topsy-turvy

Not a portion of grain, not a billboard
Not for you, not for me, no firewood for him
Water freezes to ice: is it mountainous or feather-like? Did it
need to be enforced?

SONG OF THE FOUR SEASONS OF EVENTS

Green grass on a stream bank, green grass of tomorrow
Velvety drizzle and sprouts from the bottom of the heart
However you hoe it, you can't hoe it all, said Xiao Hong

Release of fluid needs to be dealt with, thriving and forthright;
Mixing profundity with blessedness of forgetting
Crumbling of sediment; only wind wonders at veins of lotus leaves

Settle accounts and reap the relevance of past and future
The line written at this time picks apart this very time
Hide in a grape arbor and savor the non-doing of clouds

Can't follow this soap opera or guess the party boss' plots
Can't avoid river muck or hear the headman's words in a video
I feel the economy is no bubble; neither are citizens, or snow

WHEN ASHAMED, FALL DOWN ON THE STREET

God falls down on the street in August
rolls down some steps, an empty bowl at his knee
Two more bottles and He won't remember, He himself
already has 7.8 billion kids, and 800 million of them
are starving; umpteen millions are sick, with more on the way
So what would be fitting to fill that empty bowl?

Hurry hurry, or else they can't grow up
and won't grow well; vaccines won't take, just make them sweat
Shade trees here don't yield dates. All that empty, fancy talk
they know all about it. When you are supine on the street
can you sleep anyway? In the space of a dream, worlds can fall
Are the clouds white like flour or red like meat? Is it time now

to discuss ethics or theology? The problems bear down heavily
like mountains. So much that those who find an empty bowl
will pound drums and gongs on the street. The startled sky
will fall by the power of their breath, and sink in the sea
So down the hatch... the bowl has gotten itself drunk
and won't let you count for much... in a panic of hunger

Dao Zi

岛子

Dao Zi, born in 1957. His real name is Wang Min. He was a professor at the Sichuan Academy of Fine Arts and the Academy of Fine Arts at Tsinghua University. He is a poet, painter and art critic. In 1997, he won the HUMAN RIGHTS WATCH Hellman/Hammett grant poetry award in the United States; in 2014, he won the MISEREOR HUNGERTUCH 2015/2016 Art Creation Award from the German Miser Social Development Foundation; in 2016, he won the KOREAN FINE ARTS ASSOCIATION [KFAA] artistic merit Award; won the New York Art Fair Outstanding Art Work Award in 2021. He is the author of *Selected Experimental Poems of Daozi, Selected Poems of Daozi* and more than ten books on art history; he has held more than 20 personal painting exhibitions at home and abroad. Currently lives and creates in Beijing and New York.

HIDDEN CORROSION

Feathered appendages hurtle themselves
Towards a transparent window

An avian creature according to geography
A bamboo cage according to genetics

Before the gate... a half acre of bloody field
In the rear courtyard... a troop of hairless apes

River of stars, in quietude
Column of smoke, even quieter

The transparent window hurtles itself
Towards feathered appendages

A bloody field...is guiltless
Feathered appendages... even more guiltless

Feathered appendages hurtle themselves
Towards a transparent window

Behind a welded-shut iron grate
An expanse of white paper is surging

SACRED IMAGE

Why do you want to paint it?
because of crimes not seen—

I have seen my flames of darkness blazing
charring paper from behind, from which leaps
an eviscerated white horse

—Fellow traveler not yet invited

The blue-armored knight has fallen asleep
The night wrestles with mist

SEVEN-STOREY LEARNING TOWER

1

Even before that phrase is uttered, knees kneel down within the
mouth
a killer lurks on the other shore, enraged by what is in the
crosshairs
Trailing rain propagates, as do reflections of angels taken
hostage

2

A group of bald-headed philosophers, sitting quietly
a Silicon Valley of knotty problems... and down at the bottom
they've buried that time-bomb of a phrase, ticking away.

3

A camphor-wood door frame gapes... at the former site of
finance
an old phoenix takes flight with clanking wingbeats; please
synchronize
with the speed of light, please dial back the pearl-tipped second
hand

So many thin-pressed pink lips, training en masse
on the high ground of slogans, and watchwords of the drill-
sergeant snake
promote lush overlapping of their most delicate scales

A head shaved by a chisel, embroidery done by an axe
one true master per generation hands down such skills
a scream in the wasteland decides the fate of birds-and-flowers

A thornbush burns, separate sentient beings are charred
heaven arches over a diluvian epoch, the land oozes arsenic
Despite an arcane text, brought by lightning to a tower's tip

Amid a chainsaw's roar, some things cannot be shaped
in jade or gold: humankind, being flawed in design, has not
yet been saved; downfall has not yet led to ascension

Wen Rong

文蓉

Wen Rong, whose real name is Dong Rongling, is a literature lover. Her ancestral home is Changle, Fujian, and she currently lives in New Jersey, USA. The cafe cook loves her work like the powerful trunk of a tree; she loves writing like the flowers and leaves adorning the branches. Her works are occasionally published in journals.

LOVE LETTER

We are growing ever thinner, living like one page
pressed against another. This page takes a winding course
that page is tracing back to a remote past
"When the world was first created
things of the earth were without names…"
That was when we sojourned
in the Classic of Mountains and Oceans[1]
tending herds along rivers, living close to unnamed beasts
sharing scallions in spring and caltrops in fall
Many things that knew our touch exist even now
huts and hedges and a garden opening onto views of hills
In a certain dream they were gathered together
page upon page… While many of the blank spots
are the silence in which we still find ourselves
drawn in freehand lines
flowing, clean, not concrete
Anyone, while resting intoxicated next to flowers
could produce a great anonymous work

[1] The Classic of Mountains and Rivers is a Han-era collection of
myths and legends which describes many chimerical beasts. (Tr.)

WE LIVE ON A LILY PAD

Don't get the idea that everyone is fooled
in truth we merely live on a water lily leaf
As big as the world is, why can't you be
a little expansive... a round bead rolls along
now and then bumps into another, merging
beads of perfect transparency
maybe gathering in a clump
or constantly changing droplets
you race along with lithe footing
in the end you live upon a lily pad

Tenderness wells up from the heart
reaches to peel a bead's surface membrane
that invisible tension holding it in place
if a bead is just going to evaporate
might as well wipe off its see-through trace

RETURN

There is no blackness sufficient to cover up the night
Not this dark spot where I sit alone, boiling a pot of white rice
Still there is someone I am waiting for
And he has headlights on his car
That poke two bright holes in the night

HOW I FEEL WHEN I SEE THE WORD "LONELINESS"

In my cramped little room, I run into trouble
when the sail of language is raised too suddenly
We need to talk from at least a lake's breadth away
letting the boat's wake spread to bank-side sedge
through a bluebird's song, and dawn air's lingering freshness,
and having passed through their filter of gossamer fineness
to lightly let written words fall, as exquisite as morning light
If the fury of a wild storm should force us
to hole up in my cramped little room
I would not lightly tread the last few steps toward you
for the beauty of distance is best sensed among the ranks of exiles
those planted in history's deep places
on yellowed rice paper or silk
whose orchids bloom behind a plate of bullet-proof glass
Now between us two, driven to this plight by rough weather
here in this narrow little room, where the space of this lake
has been opened, by us, with the rocks placed along its shore
and plantings of shrubbery, all of them are slowly heading
towards time's millstone, in such a way
that the whole will never again be divided

AN UNFINISHED MELODY

In the first half of life, I prettified everything with language
Now is much better
Now that I am standing like a sturdy tree
simply turning about is like putting forth flowers

Chu Hong

楚鸿

Lives in New York and works as an English editor for an international news agency. Member of Overseas Chinese Writers PEN Association. She is the author of the poetry collection "Soliloquy of Age" and has published works in various literary journals, including "Vineyard Poetry Magazine", "Cross-Strait Poetry", "Hong Kong Literature", "First Line New York", "New World Poetry Magazine", MAYDAY Magazine, etc. Her works have also been published in major Chinese newspapers and periodicals in North America and Asia. Her poems and prose have been selected into more than ten poetry anthologies at home and abroad.

AWAKE!

In the nest of a tree that aims at the sky
Awake!
Surrounded by steel towers sheathed in glass
Awake!
Amid fog not dispelled by waters of Shen River
Awake!
Stared at by the plague demon's red-rimmed eyes
Awake!

There is nowhere to avoid looking it straight in the eye
Both sides are looking daggers, pushing against each other

Beside concrete containers stacked on end
Awake!
Among hills bulldozed flat and drained lakes
Awake!
In a city under snow drifts or hazy from wildfires
Awake!
In the tug-of-war between God and Buddha
Awake!

I hear a person open his mouth, only to sigh
I see a person open her eyes, only to close them

April 2023

YEAR OF THE DRAGON

Having managed......to get through
another round of expectant readiness for ripening
the pride of harvest has not yet turned up in vision's circle
Airborne dust opportunely veils my crawling heart rate
All I can do is shift to a lower musical key:
As scabbed-over hopes
climb over time's boundary marker
they are likely to grow new sprouts

Fireworks gladly test if snow will gravitate to snow*
In tragicomedies, after breaking through a blockade
one invariably hankers for a distant view
In legends a wonder-beast turns its head this way and that
to arbitrate the thousand–year clash of nimble wits
Whether favorable or not
all return to the same origin point

Moonlight leads the way with equidistant dotted lines
leveling out various attempts
no matter how slanted the starting line
only dreams really know the proper season
The zephyr comes in an understanding way
blocking the freezing rain outside your threshold

*Note: In Chinese, "snow" is sometimes used metaphorically to mean
redress of false slander or miscarried justice. (Tr.)

AN UNSEASONABLE AFTERNOON

A sprayer at the edge of a building
raises wisps of water molecules into view, wordlessly
imitating the sighs of humans who strive to be first
Brightness barges in through a window
to dispel the paralyzed limbs of weariness
but the one who wakens has no wish to decode
the subliminal hints in chaotic dreams
no longer wondering which person or which place
Whether to add marks to a calendar is a question
that does not seem suited to such an afternoon
Ambulances on all sides make screams that pierce
both the ears and the heart
At this point it becomes clear
the despair that constricts the throat
is a betrayal of springtime
The time has come: from behind goggles
uncanny human eyes are starting to assess
the trustworthiness of other living things
beginning from one's heartbeat and manner of speech
beginning from an unseasonable afternoon

March 2020, during Covid-19's initial phase in New York City

IN THE BEATING HEART OF AUTUMN

A roiling tumult of colors
comes surging towards us
stealing away our breath

Light and shadow are tossing
around one who hurtles into depths
of a tunnel made out of riotous colors
Celestial and terrestrial eternity bestow
moments of enduring life on me and you

Reality is outside the window, and a hammer blow
may be no more than the activation of a button
You and I do not touch it,
allowing a gaze
to linger devotedly
and hillside mist to wreathe

The heart of fall has been poured full
of a season's bounty, as well as its blues
With sweeping arms we muscle our way
heading forward through the sky's bottom layer

October 2022

Fir Tree

冷杉

Fir Tree, young poet. Born in Taizhou, Zhejiang, she lived in Hangzhou, Suzhou, Maryland, and Michigan. Master's degree in classical Chinese literature from Zhejiang University. Her research direction is the literature of Pre-Qin, Han, Wei, Jin, Southern and Northern Dynasties. Worked as a reporter, editor, and freelance writer. Some of her Chinese and English poems have been published in Chinese and American literary journals, and she has published a collection of poems called *Plantain Herb*.

GRAY EYES

I don't know when I first noticed it
the pupils of Grandma's eyes began fading
By the time she left us, their color settled on somber gray
they never got paler than that

After saying goodbye she kept us in mind
On certain days she would let herself be seen
not making a sound, not preceded by signs
In the vegetable garden in June, our holiday kitchen
an afternoon when rain ran from the eaves in a beaded curtain
She was immersed in her tasks, just as before
except that she no longer spoke with us
Sometimes her shadow trailed her, sometimes not

Some evenings when I feared walking alone
she would walk ahead of me, parting the dusk.
Birds were cooing in pitch black trees, their wings
dissolved in the nighttime southern breeze
The lane was reduced to a strand so tenuous
that buildings along the way disappeared
By afterglow I could see was carrying something
but I was never able
to make out what it was

Was it a hat, her folded coat, or her cherished jug?
I could not say for sure

Finally one day she stopped walking
in a spot where memory had almost died away
The visual details were like snow on a TV screen
that was losing its signal... I tried to walk
around to the front, to get a look
at what she held in her arms, but to no avail

I could only see
my gray-eyed Grandma, her eyes
as gray as a pigeon, slightly paler than roof tiles
but darker than foliage at twilight

COLD MOON

Outlander, for you these storeyed night palaces were raised
dimness for the foe and light for us…
Your solitude falls like ripe fruit, no one picks it up
O bitter toosendan fruit: peel it, squeeze it, press it
Its cry is not invasive, as was proven by the sweet dreams
of a baby. Do not worry, someday he will pay respects
to a tooth buried in an unmarked grave,* and will clasp
a white curtain's edge where a window opens to a cold moon

Go without stopping. Beside the river is a plaza, a crystal manor
sending out streaks of light; tongues of flame hiss in a dark alley,
Don't stop, shake off the clinging daylight terror behind you
avoid the sharp-eyed sniper who waylays you with fatigue
Don't stop, pass over a pedestrian bridge, through a passageway
use the coiled force of a chip to turn back a relentless turnstile
Ten, nine, eight, seven, six, five, four…
The city's beast population is going to be closed off;
now everyone draws in their oars. Look, a flock of gray owls
flies up in Central Park; at the tip of a broadcasting tower
see the cold moon.

*Note: [1] In 1641, the army officer Li Kecong was sent on a
campaign against the rebel Li Zicheng, in hopes of protecting the last Ming
emperor, Chongzhen. The campaign was clearly hopeless, and the bodies
of the dead would be difficult to recover. Before setting out, Li Kecong
yanked out a tooth, gave it to his wife, and told her to place it in a grave
where his son could someday pay respects to him. In the story told of this
event, the grave prepared for him was called a "tooth grave." (Tr.)

THE FEVERED CITY

I have smelled its swampy breath
and seen the rust of its immersion in despair—
those machines that roared awhile, then fell lastingly silent.
Once I went by way of its bulging strawberry tongue
to arrive at the darkness of its appendix
I searched for the shield shape at an exit—
that exit leading to utter filth,
an exit that I alone know.

A nightingale will await me there:
there is such purity in its notes of song
that the miasma cannot sully.

Purity akin to twilight.
With the glint of steel looming
on its horripilating hide.

On a plaza opening outward like a vocal tract
which is the very core of the fevered city,
partake of your dinner—
Beware of nails in your bread,
respect walls, but question their coldness:
Why did fire destroy those crystal lattice structures?
Why was a name smashed to pieces,
as a century toppled with it into caked dust?

Beneath a half-built Tower of Babel sleeps the rabble,
in dreams still raving that the stars here are low hanging fruit.
Moonlight pickled in preservative,
seemingly bent on destruction, casts a withering gaze
enough to flatten the lumpy mass of living things.

BLACK LASSO

Heading down the road of a childhood afternoon
in my mind a lasso of black rope is worn smooth,
each day growing thinner, like an invalid's throat—
Time, its sole ailment, keeps closing in.
Memory is the hushed rustle of snowflakes,
but also a pomegranate tree under hot sun,
and flower-skirts make a "whish" like cicada wings.

Lying by a road in youth, drifting clouds churn one's vision.
Sultry thermal currents from the sea; massive tonnage
of empty village ennui, ignited and flung skywards,
pervading the air like fireworks, and teeth often clenched
from summer bugs on the scalp,
when they started their metallic whine.
The black lasso that bound all living things
opened to release the growth of thick black fuzz.

The good earth: a requiem that merges green and gold
python-like matrix studded with cadaver spots of oleander
many corners unfrequented, like bygone days—
All those thirsty, weary, superfluous book pages
and precocious flesh pounded down by one's own strength.
Urgent wind of conspiracy theory twanging beams of light.
Dullness of flocking ducks playing in the water,
about to mount to the height of faraway peaks.

At this moment, as a leftover page of childhood
sits here with images that may combust at any moment:
"You were having a dream that belonged to other people,
even before facing an opponent, you were utterly defeated."

Wang Jian

王键

Wang Jian, born in Huanggang City, Hubei Province in 1965, is a poet. He began writing poetry and publishing works in the 1980s, and became a famous poet at universities in Wuhan. His works are scattered in Chinese and foreign poetry publications, and he has published poetry collections *Stranger* and *Dancing in Paperclips.* Since 2018, he has been the chief editor of the poetry anthology *Mountains and Lakes Collection* of Zhongnan University of Economics and Law. He now lives in New York.

SNOW OF DECEMBER

The snow is falling as ardently as fire
opening the final doorway of a secret chamber
The space of imagination has snow's luminosity
in a corridor where hope and despair are grappling
The suspense of events is hung up to receive a flogging
Only snow answers all this with its continuous fall
From its secret chamber it enters a living room
even into water that someone boils for tea
Finally, snow covers the pallid insufficiency of thought
It can impart humility and truthfulness
All things are speechless, sentience is breathless
the world leans in and listens to snow's whisper
If possible, the best thing to do right now
is to enter snow's interior, to listen
to the footfalls of its silent dance

DANCING IN A PAPER CLIP

Within a paper clip that clasped God and a dancer
the curve unfolds a drama of contesting forces
tyrants and the mob, lordly persons and plebeians
all born in the same era. And a dancer on tip-toes
tests the bottom line of a syringe. In the cloud picture
of the character hui,* he begins to dance;
with arms reaching upwards, tugging at
the black line that runs through a nebula; he tries
to drag down a galaxy's pillar of fire
his whirling legs are circling in parallel
entangled quanta tracing a labyrinthine escape
O Lord, we possess so much:
please replenish our abundant poverty
please act to release the slaves of freedom
and fill in the cracks in light-rays with light. May moonlight
and sweat give the dancer strength over suffering
Let him spin across earth with his relentless burden
in graceful, enticing curves, from starting point
back to starting point, in a story cycle like a mantra
Right then, the Hudson River, like a big paper clip
is clasped at Manhattan's neck. and in the Orient
nine bends of the Yellow River entwine the good earth's moans
Starlight over my head descends on a red lawn mower
I want to get it running, from sunrise to sunset
let stifling air be roiled by that roaring machine
let the whirling blade roll over the garden's thick weeds

*Note: The Chinese word for paper clip is 迴紋針 (huiwen-zhen), literally means "needle that has a winding pattern." The word 回/迴 in ancient seal script looks like a wisp of cloud. (Tr.)

HEADING INTO STILLNESS

In the noisy, disordered, raucous world
I tilt towards the stillness

I turn on all my organs
I turn my ears, eyes and nose
turn my hands, turn my feet
even my hair—
in the direction of stillness

In a time of blooming flowers, a fallen leaf has a wish
The measure of evolution for all living things
takes place somewhere unseen
in the smallest increments
in the direction of stillness

I draw near to a poem
I draw near to a lyric of fury
and it carries me along
like a seed that goes airborne in spring
in the direction of stillness

I see a giraffe placing a child up in a tree
then its head plunges into a bucket of water
I see quanta having a dialogue over a span of two light years
I observe and see a maple leaf on the ground

and the flight it would take returning to a treetop
in the direction of stillness

In April, in Ukraine
a shoulder-fired missile locks onto its target
right when an artillery shell lands
both of them are headed in the same direction

towards stillness

A SHOE WAITING TO GO OUTSIDE

It shows signs of exposure to snow, and to mud
from the bottom of the Red Sea

It shows weariness on its features
and a haggard look

Open its laced-up front to the air, let its sweat
flow freely, let light shine in to dry it
like an old creature in the sunlight
that slows its breathing when asleep

Like an infant returned to the womb
in a curled position that does away with
the wrinkles on its body

You are turned to face the front door, despite
your smudged and dusty visage, ready for
a new departure at any time

Though your other half that was beside you always
may have gone missing

Surely it too travels a wanderer's road

Yan Li

严力

Poet and artist, Yan Li was born in Beijing in 1954. He started writing poetry in 1973 and painting in 1979. He was a member of the Beijing avant-garde art group "Stars Painting Group" and the literary group "Today" in 1979. In 1984, the earliest personal exhibition of avant-garde art in China was held in the Shanghai People's Park Exhibition Hall. In 1985, he came to study in the United States from Beijing and founded the "First Line New York" poetry magazine in New York in 1987 (it ceased publication in 2000). In June 2019, "First Line New York" magazine resumed publication in New York. He continues to serve as editor-in-chief. In 2018, he served as the chairman of the Flushing Poetry Festival in New York. In the same year, he became the president of the Overseas Chinese Writers Abroad in New York.

CHOPSTICKS

I am a pair of chopsticks
I have gone through an era of starvation
by licking myself I learned what sufficiency is
In a thriving era it took the dishes of many cooks
to make up for what my tongue tip once lacked
Now I savor the Way of caring for the body
so I try to end my dinners at 70% full
In fact, the longevity of chopsticks
is not a matter of ultimate concern
because chopsticks can only be alive
for the length of time they are in use
That being so, on certain occasions
if fate decrees that I am faced
with a whole steak sizzling in a pan
these chopsticks can quickly adapt
to the apt use of a knife and fork

After all, this pair of chopsticks knows the score
Yesterday, the Chinese language hosted a lunch
When one chopstick, whose name is "I"
let loose with an exaggerated belch
the other chopstick, whose name is "Myself,"
reacted with an offended glare

POLEMICAL WAR

Depending on where you've gotten to now
your downward gaze will be fixed on the screen
of a mobile phone or an unmanned drone

The area which you cannot reach
is beyond the scope of cognition
There is no pre-established data there
to feed the generative routines of AI

And so, wherever you get to tomorrow
you will find no scenes of a brave new world
or an algorithm able to yield humanistic fruits

Go on climbing, along with your weapons
even further up the pattern of a branching tree
being able to produce these blooms, such as they are
must have been quite a feat for weaklings

EXCEPT FOR

Within the human body
except for what is eaten
there are no fields or orchards…
Except for what is drunk
there are no lakes, no rivers
Except for desire
no churches or temples
Except for imagination
no cloudscapes or constellations
Except for wearing down and aging
no seasonal change or reincarnation
Except for illness no bankruptcy
Except for limits no limitlessness

In the land where bodies live
except for male and female parts
there are no remote regions

COUNTRYMEN

The ailment called "countrymen" has been
under treatment for thousands of years
but starting today
all surgical procedures will need to be utilized
to remove from the patients' bodies
that operating theater called "the nation"

This notification comes from outer space
My countrymen can't make out its meaning
except for in this poem

October 2022

FLYING

I've always liked to watch birds flying
also airplanes with their outstretched wings
or maybe clouds floating through the sky

After many years I finally realized
no matter what the criterion
only the wind can be called
the supreme master of flying
for only the wind, after colliding against buildings
against mountains and even the ground underfoot
it is still able to fly

BITTER COFFEE

Weak rays of sunlight
come to my window at 8:00 a.m.
I can even sense
the haze retreating into the earth
I savor last night's dreams
which roughly belong to two kinds
just like the smog and the sunlight
I stretch my arms and roll my neck
raise a bitter morning coffee to my lips
As for the sugar and cream, they are in my body
already deposited there, over many years, by Mother

May 14, 2023 (Mother's Day)

Lü De'an

吕德安

Born March 18, 1960. He is a poet and painter. In 1981 he graduated from Fujian's Art Academy. In the early 1980s, along with the poet and painter, Tong Ren, he established the Friday Poetry Society and became an important member of the Nanjing poetry society, "They". During this period, he published the poetry collections, *Paper Snake, The Other Half of Life,* and *The South to the North.* He moved to New York in 1992 and made his living painting. He also wrote the long poem, "Mankato." In 1994, he won the "They" Poetry Prize. That same year, he built a residence in the mountains of his hometown in Fujian, and wrote the long poem, "Right Where One Belongs". He also devoted a great deal of time to painting, and participated in Mou Sen's Theater Workshop in Beijing. He went abroad again in 1998. During this period he published his poetry collection, *Obstinate Stones,* and in 2011 he published his collection, *Right Where One Belongs.* That same year he won the Yunnan Gaoligong Poetry Prize, and also established Fujian's "Friday Painting Society." In 2012 he became a poetry moderator of the website, Impact China. He currently resides in Beijing where he devotes his time to painting.

MANHATTAN AND ROOSEVELT ISLAND

Between Manhattan Island
and Roosevelt Island at night…
if a gigantic seagull
were to glide over soundlessly…

breathlessly; and if it were
a windy, snowy evening
I wouldn't know if that lost gull
were acting on a moment's impulse

Here we have two lit-up boroughs
between them, a steadily shrinking sea
Here in the night, is that gull
simply adapting, learning how

to exist between shafts of light
or is it borrowing the dim light and snow
to pursue a school of fish in the darkness?
If so, I hope its wish is fulfilled

If I discover to my surprise the whiteness
of the underarms beneath its wings
I will have found my the color of my loneliness
between Manhattan and Roosevelt islands

Zhou Defang

周德芳

Poet, writer, senior media professional. Formerly served as a reporter for Anhui Daily, Hainan Legal Daily, and deputy editor in chief of Shanghai DVD Guide, Special Digest, and World News for Wanjiang Business Daily. Poetry, prose, reportage, and other works have been published in Hong Kong Poetry Journal, New York Times, People's Daily Overseas Edition, World Journal, International Daily, and Overseas Chinese Daily. Currently the chief reporter of Hanna Media in the United States and the deputy editor in chief of international poetry. A collection of poems and essays titled 'Fragrant Grass in the End of the World' has been published. Settle in New York.

I HAVE A DATE WITH MAPLE LEAVES

I have a rendezvous with maple leaves
to meet again on time's magpie bridge [1]
the reincarnation of autumn
is spread across October's sky
A once-a-year rendezvous
is dipped in a sunlit rainbow
A wanton maiden's dreams in a bower
Are vying in riotous, mottled colors
Fall briskness stirs the lissomeness
of a girl-goddess; her marmoreal feet
trip along in brisk wafts of flower scent

A red Ormosa seed tells of pining in the southland
a maple leaf confides ardor from the northern borders
Green is fleeing a chilled leaf, yet it whispers of golden fall
I cast off everything, seek the scent it breathes into the air
To embrace a maple leaf is to fuse with an intriguing soul
The flame of love leaps and pervades the space around
Lift the knapsack of poetry onto your shoulders
keep me company in pacing about and wandering

I hereby keep a lifelong promise to a maple leaf
what is more, I conduct this as a ceremony of love
In this ocean of fiery redness
Every maple tree shows gratitude

for the creator's gifts, deft and intricate

for prayers said by every stamen and pistil

The eyes of the beloved no longer stray far

all wounds can be soothed by this love

[1] *This alludes to the myth of Cowherd and Weaver Maid. After escaping from a palace in Heaven she came to earth and fell in love with Cowherd. The two were separated and only allowed to meet each other once a year, on a bridge of magpies spanning the great Sky River. (Tr.)*

www.ingramcontent.com/pod-product-compliance
Lightning Source LLC
Chambersburg PA
CBHW020401130626
46549CB00006B/2381